VINTAGE

VINTAGE

CALIFORNIA WINE LABELS

OF THE 1930s

Edited by Christopher Miya and Ashley Ingram
Foreword by Frances Dinkelspiel
Introduction by Marie Silva

Heyday, Berkeley, California
California Historical Society, San Francisco, California

The labels reproduced in this book can be found in the California Historical Society's Kemble Collections on Western Printing and Publishing. Established through gifts from George Laban Harding, the Kemble Collections consist of more than four thousand volumes, extensive pamphlet and ephemeral materials, files of more than three hundred periodicals, and significant manuscript holdings, all pertaining to the history of printing and publishing, with special emphasis on California and the West. This book is published in conjunction with an exhibition featuring the Lehmann Printing wine, beer, and spirits labels at the California Historical Society, December 2016–January 2017.

Library of Congress Control Number: 2016946105

Cover and Interior Design: Ashley Ingram

This book was copublished with the California Historical Society. Orders, inquiries, and correspondence should be addressed to:
Heyday
P.O. Box 9145, Berkeley, CA 94709
(510) 549-3564, Fax (510) 549-1889
www.heydaybooks.com

Printed in Visalia, CA, by Jostens

10 9 8 7 6 5 4 3 2 1

FOREWORD

Frances Dinkelspiel

The colorful wine labels of the 1930s showcased in this book might puzzle today's wine lovers. The varietals and geographic names on the labels bear little resemblance to what is popular today. Instead of Cabernet Sauvignon or Chardonnay, the labels offer up California Ruby Port, California Burgundy, Angelica, and Tokay. The wines aren't from familiar locales, like Napa and Sonoma, either, but from towns named Tulare, Martinez, Selma.

These labels hark back to a dark time in the California wine industry at the height of the Great Depression, shortly after Prohibition had ended. Their bucolic scenes and titles invoking royalty were an invitation to set troubles aside and find cheer in a glass. Unfortunately, few could enjoy what they sipped. Most of the wine made in California in the 1930s was downright awful. It was sweet and strong and mass produced from low-quality grapes.

The lackluster plonk was a legacy of Prohibition, which had decimated a once-robust industry. Before the Eighteenth Amendment went into effect on January 16, 1920, California had more than seven hundred wineries and hundreds of thousands of acres of vineyards. The state exported millions of gallons of wine around the world, and some of its bottles had earned gold medals in Europe. The California Wine Association, a virtual monopoly that controlled 80 percent of the state's wine production and distribution, dominated much of the wine trade. Its Winehaven, on the edge of San Francisco Bay at Point Molate near Richmond, was the world's largest wine production facility.

When selling alcoholic beverages became illegal, more than five hundred wineries shut down. A few survived the fourteen-year ban by selling sacramental wine to priests or rabbis, or "tonics" to doctors who prescribed wine for medicinal purposes. A number of wineries managed to thrive for a few years because of a loophole in the law that permitted the head of each household to make up to two hundred gallons of wine each year. Suddenly, there was a huge demand for fresh grapes throughout the United States. When boxcars carrying California grapes pulled into rail stations in New York City or Philadelphia, hordes of men would rush to bid on the flats of fruit. Grapes that went for $10 a ton before Prohibition suddenly sold for $75 to $100 a ton.

But most fine wine grapes didn't fare well on long train trips, so ambitious growers ripped out their vines and planted hearty, thick-skinned grape varieties such as ruby-red Alicante Bouschet or the table grape Flame Tokay—an action that would eventually haunt them. In the first six years of Prohibition, vineyard plantings actually doubled in California, only to shrink after the market for fresh grapes collapsed in 1926 because of overproduction.

When Repeal came on December 5, 1933, many people were optimistic that the wine industry would spring back to life. One of the top stories in *The Healdsburg Tribune* that week heralded the first legal shipment of wine in years: five carloads, worth more than $75,000 (or $1.4 million in 2016 dollars), had left the area. (The winery had made the wine in anticipation of

Repeal.) Another winery immediately put fifty men to work bottling wine and another twenty women to glue on labels, the paper reported.

But the hoped-for revival didn't happen, at least not for many decades. The Depression meant there was no money and little credit to buy and restore abandoned wineries, or to replace rusted wine presses, rotted casks, and other winemaking equipment. Few experienced winemakers remained, leaving eager novices and speculators who didn't know what they were doing to revive the almost-dormant industry.

The biggest problem was that the majority of the grapes in California were ill suited for making wine. The thick-skinned varieties that traveled so well didn't produce a wine with flavor and balance. Neither did the table and raisin grapes that covered much of the Central Valley. But wine was made from them anyway.

The results were dismal. When Maynard A. Joslyn, an instructor in the College of Agriculture at the University of California, Berkeley, toured the wineries that had started up in California after Repeal, he didn't find one that produced decent wine. "I've never tasted so many mousy, turned wines," he recalled years later. "These wines were spoiled."

One way the winemakers disguised their mediocre product was by fortifying it with neutral spirits or brandy, which produced a sweet and intoxicating beverage that was 20 percent alcohol, significantly higher than the 13 percent alcohol level found in most dry table wines. The sweet wine was extremely popular and vastly outsold dry red table wine. The wine was made in huge batches, often under less than pristine conditions, and shipped in bulk around the country, where individual distributors and retailers bottled it and affixed their own labels. Unlike today, few individual wineries bottled their own products.

Since most Americans had gotten out of the habit of drinking bottled wine, distributors used names derived from familiar European regions, such as Chianti or Burgundy, or semi-generic names like Claret, Chablis, Port, or Sherry. A few wines specified grape varietals such as Tokay or Riesling, but usually the wine found in those bottles had no connection with the name. They were just white wines sweetened with Muscat.

The labels, then, served to entice consumers, to lure them into buying something that wasn't delivered in the bottle. Notice the number of royal names, such as "Old King Cole," "Kings and Queens," and "Royal Knight." Or terms evoking the California Gold Rush. There are pictures of vineyards and mountains and wagons loaded with luscious red grapes, as well as the god Bacchus turning a wine press.

This kind of labeling, according to James T. Lapsley, a historian of the Napa Valley, gave bulk wine a "patina of quality" and made the producers feel better about the inferior wines they were pushing on the public.

The reliance on bulk generic wines with colorful but non-specific labels started to change in the 1960s as an increasing number of ambitious winemakers aimed to make higher-quality wine. They began to plant better-quality grapes, such as Cabernet Sauvignon and Chardonnay (although California wine was made from equal amounts of wine and table grapes as late as 1961). They paid closer attention to how wine was fermented, aged, and bottled. American tastes began to shift, too, as jet travel made visiting Europe easier and Julia Child's best-selling cookbook brought French cuisine, and the notion of drinking wine with dinner, into U.S. homes.

In 1967, thirty-four years after Prohibition ended, dry table wines finally overtook sweet fortified wines in popularity, signaling a shift that has continued until today. Consumers gravitated at first to jug wines like Gallo Hearty Burgundy or Carlo Rossi Chablis. As their tastes evolved—and wine marketing improved—they embraced the 750-milliliter bottles that held wines from distinct viticulture areas such as Oakville, Rutherford, Dry Creek Valley, or the Sonoma Coast. Wine labels soon detailed what kinds of grapes were used, where they were grown, and which winery made the wine. While that trend provides a more accurate accounting of the wine inside a bottle, many of today's labels lack the whimsy of those from the 1930s.

INTRODUCTION

Marie Silva

Like many of life's sweetest pleasures, the vintage labels in this book were discovered in an unlikely place, tucked unassumingly between folders of more contemporary (and less captivating) wine labels collected for the California Historical Society in the 1970s and 1980s. Although the provenance of the collection was unknown, most of the Great Depression—era specimens— in their endlessly creative reworking of like design elements— clearly shared a common paternity. A little digging revealed that these exquisite labels were manufactured on an undeniably mass scale by one of the country's largest label plants, the now-forgotten Lehmann Printing and Lithographing Company of San Francisco. During a period of terrible privation and unrest, Lehmann's labels graced hundreds of thousands of bottles of mass-manufactured, highly alcoholic wines and liquors, invoking in brilliant color deliciously unrealistic fantasies of peace, plenty, and the high-class life. Marrying design with consumer ideology, the Lehmann oeuvre represents a forgotten high point of American commercial art.

The history of the Lehmann Printing and Lithographing Company is sadly underdocumented, surprisingly so given the firm's boasted success. Founded in 1911 by Adolph Lehmann with an initial investment of $190, the firm expanded into a major industrial printing operation valued at $600,000 by 1935. Referred to as "the printer who hasn't heard about the depression" by a dazzled correspondent for the *Inland Printer*,

Lehmann employed a staff of one hundred people, including a permanent staff of artists who designed each custom label with skillful care. Although Lehmann took personal responsibility for every label, it was his artists, toiling in anonymity and working overtime to fulfill an avalanche of orders, who assured that the Lehmann product met the highest standards of quality in concept, design, and execution. Lehmann seemed to interpret his own life story in Horatio Alger terms; after all, he was the son of German immigrants with only a grammar-school education who worked his way up from errand boy to become sole owner of an internationally renowned printing firm. Yet his labels tell another, surprising story: one of anonymous and collective effort coupled with endless and uncredited artistic innovation.

Although each Lehmann label is a marvel of design in its own right, the labels in this book are not "artisanal" in the contemporary sense. In today's artisanal culture, the individual creator is prominent, inscribing his or her personal identity on each unique, handcrafted product. In contrast, the stamps on Lehmann's labels remind us that these beautiful ephemera were mass produced, with figures of 50 and 75 representing lots of 50,000 and 75,000 labels. In 1934, orders from three large wineries totaled over $100,000 (nearly enough to cover the firm's annual payroll), a testament to the industrial scale on which both the wines and the labels were manufactured. To meet an ever-increasing demand for labels, Lehmann pioneered a stock label service in the mid-1930s, creating catalogs of generic labels with stock vignettes that could be applied to a wide variety of products. The inventive talent of the Lehmann art department continued to shine in the firm's extraordinary output of individualized labels, including the specimens that are found in this book. Yet even custom labels shared standard colors, backgrounds (parted curtains and aging manuscripts were favorites), and lettering.

We do not typically associate mass production with the finest craftsmanship, but it was within the context of high-pressure and anonymous factory work that the Lehmann art department flourished. Like John Ruskin's Gothic artisans, these unknown workers found in their daily grind an opportunity for seemingly inexhaustible creative invention. None of the labels is attributed to an identified artist; we do not know the size of the department or the names of the individual artists who constituted it. Yet each custom label order was treated individually—not as "cheap work," in Lehmann's words, but as a unique problem with a design solution to be worked out artistically. Lehmann artists worked with a somewhat limited visual vocabulary, conforming to and elaborating on a house style that is easy to recognize but hard to define. One notices the generous use of pinks, blacks, and golds; striking and colorful juxtapositions; and weirdly effective combinations of art deco design sensibility with faux mission, medieval, or antique vignettes. Characteristic of this style are the superlative Old Cathedral brand labels: modern cursive scripts and sans serif fonts are superimposed over the ominous image of a rising "old cathedral" that looks remarkably like an art deco skyscraper.

Lehmann believed that a good label was the expression of an idea, conceived and executed with a specific purpose. In his labels, these ideas were expressed in recurring motifs—the theater curtain and top hat; the chivalric knight and kindly friar; the heavy vine, peaceful field, and magnificent chateau;

the racehorse and yacht—whose purpose might be understood as the marketing of the California myth. A beautiful and unsettling example is the Varsity brand California Tokay label designed for Los Angeles's Hollenbeck Beverage Company. Two framed vignettes show a padre blessing a kneeling Indian and an oddly modern-looking mission complex. These appear against a classic Lehmann manuscript background, decorated with orderly fields and a plump cluster of grapes, on which the incongruously collegiate brand name, Varsity, is printed in ornate Gothic lettering. The label mythologizes both California's past and its present, illustrating a vision of racial and industrial harmony from which the bitter realities of history are excluded. (Old Dixie is similarly and wistfully invoked in whiskey labels that celebrate the idle comfort of the slaveholding class.) Again and again, as great strikes rocked both rural and urban California, Lehmann's artist workers turned to a romanticized past—the Middle Ages, the Mission Era, even the antebellum South—for inspiration. The beautiful images they created give us pleasure and give us pause. As I admire the extraordinary artistry and inventiveness of the Lehmann product, I also wonder: what contradictions lie in the glittering gadgets of our own design-driven age?

SIMI

CALIFORNIA
PINK CHAMPAGNE
BULK PROCESS
NATURAL FERMENTATION

SPARKLING   WINE

PRODUCED AND BOTTLED BY
SIMI WINERIES, HEALDSBURG, SONOMA CO., CALIFORNIA
ALCOHOL 13% BY VOLUME · 1 PT. 10 FL. OZ.

CONTENTS
13 FL. OZ.
ALCOHOL 12%
BY VOLUME

ESTAB 1890

JEAN BART
BRAND

California

PINK CHAMPAGNE
BULK PROCESS

Naturally Fermented

SPARKLING 50 WINE

DEMI-SEC

PRODUCED AND BOTTLED BY
CELLA WINE COMPANY
FRESNO, CALIFORNIA

LEHMANN, S.F.

CHARMAT

BRAND

ALCOHOL 12% BY VOLUME   1 PT. 10 FL. OZS.

25 *Sparkling Wine*

CALIFORNIA PINK
CHAMPAGNE

Bulk Process

PRODUCED AND BOTTLED BY

CELLA WINE COMPANY

BONDED WINERY 3612 — FRESNO, CALIFORNIA

LEHMANN, S.F.

CAL-SEC

CALIFORNIA
CHAMPAGNE

NATURALLY FERMENTED
BY BULK PROCESS

ALCOHOL 12%
BY VOLUME

Pink Label

50

EXTRA
DRY

Sparkling Wine

NET CONTENTS
1 PT. 10 FL.OZS.

★

PRODUCED AND BOTTLED BY
CELLA WINE COMPANY
BONDED WINERY 3612 — FRESNO, CALIFORNIA

LEHMANN S.F.

CONTENTS
8 FL. OZS.
ALCOHOL 12%
BY VOLUME

25

JEAN BART

BRAND

California

CHAMPAGNE

BULK PROCESS

Naturally Fermented

DEMI-SEC

PRODUCED AND BOTTLED BY

CELLA WINE COMPANY

FRESNO, CALIFORNIA

LEHMANN, S.F.

GOLD MEDALS

TURIN 1911 · MILAN 1906 · DUBLIN 1892 · CHICAGO 1893 · SAN FRANCISCO 1894

TRADE
REG.U.S.

MARK
PAT.OFF.

ASTI & TURIN 1898 · PARIS 1900 · BORDEAUX 1895 · BUFFALO 1901 · ST.LOUIS 1904 · LEWIS & CLARK 1905

ITALIAN SWISS COLONY

NET CONTENTS
1 PT. 10 FL. OZS.

ALCOHOL 12%
BY VOLUME

50

CALIFORNIA CHAMPAGNE
NATURALLY FERMENTED IN THE BOTTLE

Asti Special Dry

BOTTLED FOR
ITALIAN SWISS COLONY
EXPORT DIVISION

Asti, Cal.

LEHMANN, S.F.

GOLD TREASURE

CALIFORNIA
MELLOW
SHERRY

50 *A Rare Wine*

ESPECIALLY

PACKED FOR

CONNOISSEURS

PRODUCED AND BOTTLED BY
THE ELK GROVE WINERY, INC.
ELK GROVE, CALIFORNIA

for

L'HERMITAGE-ELK GROVE
ELK GROVE, CALIFORNIA

TAX PAID BY STAMPS AFFIXED TO CASE

CONTENTS ONE QUART

SPECIAL **D** SELECTION

Dunhill

25

CALIFORNIA
DRY SHERRY

A Rare

Wine

ESPECIALLY PACKED
FOR CONNOISSEURS

•

Produced
and Bottled at the
winery in California by
ELK GROVE WINERY, INC.
ELK GROVE, CALIFORNIA

•

ALCOHOL 20%
BY VOLUME

A Rare Wine

PRODUCED AND BOTTLED BY
ELK GROVE WINERY, ELK GROVE, CALIFORNIA

50

California

ALCOHOL 20% BY VOLUME

Mellow Sherry Wine

Mellow Sherry Wine

EXOTA

EXQUISITE

T. M REG.

BRAND

CALIFORNIA
SHERRY WINE

ALCOHOL 20% BY VOLUME

BOTTLED BY
DISTILLERS OUTLET CO,
LOS ANGELES, CALIFORNIA

LEHMANN, S. F.

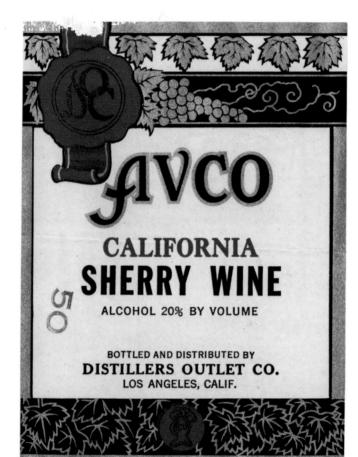

AVCO

CALIFORNIA
SHERRY WINE

ALCOHOL 20% BY VOLUME

BOTTLED AND DISTRIBUTED BY
DISTILLERS OUTLET CO.
LOS ANGELES, CALIF.

I.C.M.

NET
CONTENTS

ONE
GALLON

SELECTED

STOCK

WITHDRAWN
FROM TAX PAID
CONTAINER

OVER 19% AND NOT
OVER 21% ALCOHOL
BY VOLUME

TRADE MARK

CALIFORNIA

50

SHERRY

WINE

Meda Bros.

SACRAMENTO   CALIFORNIA

Pride of Livermore

DRAWN FROM TAX
PAID CONTAINER

ALCOHOLIC STRENGTH
NOT OVER 20%

CALIFORNIA

Sherry 50

WINE

NET CONTENTS 1 QUART

CRYSTAL WINE CO.
LIVERMORE, CAL.
o
SOLE DISTRIBUTORS
HAYWARD BOTTLING CO.
HAYWARD, CAL.

Siesta

CALIFORNIA

Sherry

ALCOHOL 20% BY VOL.
BOTTLED BY

MOUNT ST. JOHN WINERY

OAKVILLE, CALIFORNIA

Old Sacramento

Brand

CALIFORNIA

Mellow Sherry

PRODUCED AND BOTTLED
AT THE WINERY BY

Elk Grove Winery, Inc.

ELK GROVE, CALIFORNIA

ALCOHOL 20% BY VOLUME

BOTTLED IN CALIFORNIA

75

CALIFORNIA GROWERS
BRAND

CALIFORNIA PORT   CALIFORNIA SHERRY   CALIFORNIA MUSCATEL

THESE SILVER MEDALS OF AWARD WERE WON BY OUR CALIFORNIA PORT, SHERRY AND MUSCATEL
AT THE GOLDEN GATE INTERNATIONAL EXPOSITION, SAN FRANCISCO, IN 1939

CALIFORNIA
Pale Dry Sherry 75

ALCOHOL 20% BY VOLUME

PRODUCED AND BOTTLED BY

CALIFORNIA GROWERS WINERIES

CUTLER, CALIFORNIA

BOTTLED IN CALIFORNIA

CALIFORNIA

SHERRY WINE

Brannagan's
VALENCIA AT 20TH PHARMACY. SAN FRANCISCO

Smil·O

T. M. REG.

CALIFORNIA

25 Sherry Wine

ALCOHOL 20% BY VOLUME

TAX PAID BY STAMPS
AFFIXED TO CASE

BOTTLED BY **SMILO WINERIES & BOTTLING CO.** FRESNO CALIFORNIA

ELK GROVE

BRAND

CALIFORNIA
DRY SHERRY

75

ALCOHOL 20% BY VOLUME

PRODUCED AND BOTTLED BY THE
ELK GROVE WINERY, INCORPORATED
ELK GROVE   CALIFORNIA

BOTTLED AT THE WINERY

Olde Abbé

ALCOHOL
20% BY VOLUME

BRAND

CALIFORNIA
DRY SHERRY

EXTRA SPECIAL

Specially Selected

PRODUCED **AND** BOTTLED
AT THE WINERY IN CALIFORNIA

—— BY ——
ELK GROVE WINERY, INC.
ELK GROVE, CALIF.

MIRA LOMA
BRAND

BONDED
WINERY
No. 141

14TH
DISTRICT

-CALIFORNIA WINE

SHERRY 75

ALCOHOLIC CONTENT 20% BY VOLUME

NET CONTENTS ONE GALLON

BOTTLED FOR

J. S. LAZAR WHOLESALE LIQUOR CO.

SAN DIEGO, CALIFORNIA

A Product of FRUIT INDUSTRIES, LTD., Guasti, Calif.

WITHDRAWN FROM TAX PAID CONTAINER

ALCOHOL 19.5%-21% BY VOLUME

Kings and Queens

REG. U.S. PAT. OFF.

BRAND

California Sherry Wine

DRAWN OFF OR BOTTLED BY

DIXIE WINE CO.

ATLANTA, GA.   DISTRICT OF GEORGIA

FROM TAX PAID CONTAINERS RECEIVED FROM

Italian Wine Co.

LOS ANGELES, CALIF.

B. W. No. 3773   14TH DIST. CALIF.

CONTENTS ONE-HALF PINT

LEHMANN. S. F.

ALCOHOL
20% BY VOLUME

Royal Knight

CALIFORNIA
SHERRY WINE

BOTTLED AND DISTRIBUTED BY
DISTILLERS OUTLET CO.
LOS ANGELES, CALIF.

LEHMANN, S.F.

MEDA'S

CALIFORNIA WINES

Sherry

25

OVER 19% AND NOT OVER 21% ALCOHOL BY VOLUME

NET CONTENTS ONE PINT

MEDA BROTHERS

SACRAMENTO, CALIFORNIA

Rogers'
de luxe

50

BRAND

CALIFORNIA
MELLOW SHERRY

ALCOHOL 20% BY VOLUME
BOTTLED EXCLUSIVELY FOR

T. H. ROGERS
148-33 HILLSIDE AVE.
JAMAICA, NEW YORK
BY
ELK GROVE WINERY, Inc.
ELK GROVE
CALIFORNIA

SAN JUAN
BRAND

California Burgundy

ALCOHOL
13%
BY VOLUME

BOTTLED BY
GOLDEN GATE WINERY INC.
OAKLAND, CALIFORNIA
B.W. NO 1826. 14TH DIST. CALIF.

75

TAX PAID BY STAMPS AFFIXED TO CASE

DINNER BELL · DINNER BELL · DINNER BELL · DINNER BELL

HELPS MAKE A
BY GOLLY
JOLLY OLD GALLO
FATHER OF WINE
GOOD MEAL BETTER
BUY GALLO

THIS WINE IS MADE FROM GRAPES RAISED IN NORTHERN CALIFORNIA PRODUCED SOLELY FROM VINES GROWN FROM **IMPORTED CUTTINGS** ... WHICH GRAPES ARE SELECTED FOR THEIR HIGH QUALITY, COLOR, SWEETNESS AND SOUNDNESS. **NOTE ITS DISTINCTIVE FLAVOR. THIS WINE HAS BEEN ESPECIALLY PRODUCED FOR THE AMERICAN FAMILY AND HELPS MAKE A GOOD MEAL BETTER.**

DINNER BELL

SEMI-SWEET

CALIFORNIA
RED TABLE WINE

ALCOHOL 13% BY VOLUME

BOTTLED BY

GALLO WINE CO. 50

LOS ANGELES, CALIF.

PRODUCED BY E. & J. GALLO WINERY
B. W. 4213   MODESTO, CALIF.

THIS DELICIOUS WINE CAN BE SERVED CHILLED OR AT ROOM TEMPERATURE.

TRY **DINNER BELL** WHITE TABLE WINE WITH CREAM DISHES, SOUPS, SALADS, CHICKEN, FISH OR ANY MILDLY FLAVORED FOOD.

TRY **DINNER BELL RED TABLE WINE** WITH GAME, ROAST BEEF, STEAKS, TURKEY, POT ROAST, CHOPS, MACARONI AND OTHER FULL FLAVORED MEALS.

Chateau Monterey

Brand

ALCOHOL 13% BY VOLUME

CALIFORNIA
Burgundy

PRODUCED AND BOTTLED BY

CELLA WINE COMPANY

BONDED WINERY 3612 - FRESNO, CALIF.

ALCOHOL 12%
BY VOLUME

TRADE   MARK

VERO

California

Claret

MANUFACTURED AND BOTTLED BY

GOLDEN STATE WINES, INC.

SAN FRANCISCO, CALIF.

BONDED WINERY No. 3592   14TH SUP. ADM. DIST. CALIF.
TAX PAID BY STAMPS AFFIXED TO CASE

Italian Swiss Colony
FAMOUS WINES

COLONY
Special
BRAND

ALCOHOL 12%
BY VOL.

CALIFORNIA
BURGUNDY 50
BOTTLED AT THE WINERY
BY
ITALIAN SWISS COLONY
ASTI, CALIFORNIA

LEHMANN S.F.

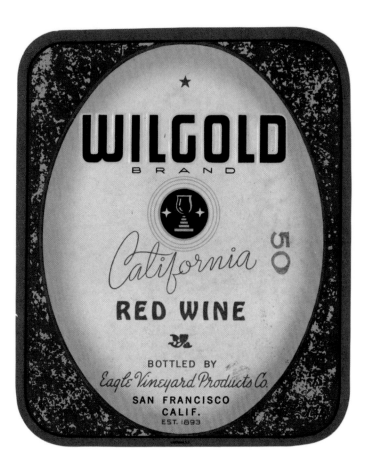

BOTTLED IN BOND

Royal Chateau

CALIFORNIA   VINTAGE

BURGUNDY 50

CONTAINS NOT OVER 4% ALCOHOL BY VOLUME

OLD ABBEY WINE CO.

NET CONTENTS 24 FL. OZS.   SAN FRANCISCO, CALIF.   BONDED WINERY NO. A-957

O-DOURO

BRAND

CALIFORNIA

Claret

WINE

ALCOHOL 13% BY VOLUME
PRODUCED AND BOTTLED BY
GONSALVES WINERY

75

BONDED WINERY NO. 4032 - 14TH DIST. - MARTINEZ, CALIFORNIA

PARROTT

Sonoma Valley

CALIFORNIA
CABERNET

ALCOHOL 12% BY VOLUME

Produced and Bottled by
Montepulciano Wineries

Healdsburg, Sonoma Co., Calif., B. W. No. 2332

Distributed by Parrott & Co., Los Angeles, Calif.

SERVE WITHOUT COOLING

La Mirada

CALIFORNIA WINE

CLARET

ALCOHOLIC CONTENT 12% TO 14% BY VOLUME

WITHDRAWN FROM TAX PAID CONTAINER

BOTTLED BY

Valley Vineyard Co.

LOS ANGELES, CALIFORNIA.

50

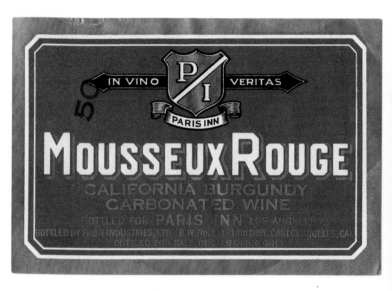

IN VINO **P I** VERITAS

PARIS INN

50

MOUSSEUX ROUGE

CALIFORNIA BURGUNDY
CARBONATED WINE

BOTTLED FOR PARIS INN LOS ANGELES

BOTTLED BY FRUIT INDUSTRIES, LTD. - B.W. No. 1 - 1 - 14th DIST. CAL. LOS ANGELES, CAL.

BOTTLED FOR SALE IN CALIFORNIA ONLY

L'HERMITAGE

BRAND

ALCOHOL
13% BY VOLUME

CALIFORNIA
ALICANTE

25

Specially Selected

PRODUCED AND BOTTLED
AT THE WINERY IN CALIFORNIA

—— BY ——

ELK GROVE WINERY. INC.
ELK GROVE, CALIF.

EL REY 50

RESERVE CALIFORNIA

WINES

CALIFORNIA
CHABLIS

ALCOHOL 13% BY VOLUME

BOTTLED BY
CALIFORNIA GROWERS
WINERIES
CUTLER, CALIFORNIA

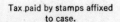
Tax paid by stamps affixed
to case.

ʃAN JUAN

Trade Mark

PURE CALIFORNIA

SAUTERNE
50 WINE

GOLDEN GATE WINERY, INC.
OAKLAND, CALIFORNIA

Net Contents 24 Ozs.
Alcohol Strength 12%-14% by Volume
11th Permissive District.   Bonded Winery 1826

Varsity Brand

CALIFORNIA 75
TOKAY
WINE

ALCOHOLIC
CONTENTS 20%
BY VOLUME

NET CONTENTS
ONE GALLON

Hollenbeck Beverage Co.
LOS ANGELES, CALIF.

DON MARCO

BOTTLED AT
BONDED WINERY
No. 22-11TH PERM.
DISTRICT, CALIF.

TAX PAID
BY STAMP AF-
FIXED TO CASE
PERMIT No.
CAL. A 803

75

CALIFORNIA

ALCOHOLIC
STRENGTH 20%
TO 21% BY VOLUME

NET
CONTENTS
1 PINT 8 OZ.

TOKAY

WINE
BOTTLED EXPRESSLY FOR
A. SCHULTE - NEW YORK
MADERA WINERIES & DISTILLERIES
K. ARAKELIAN INC.
MADERA, CALIFORNIA

NET CONTENTS 1 QUART

INDEPENDENT VINTAGE

PURE OLD CALIFORNIA

ANGELICA WINE

—

BOTTLED BY

INDEPENDENT VINTAGE
COMPANY
GLENDALE, CALIFORNIA

—

25

ALCOHOLIC CONTENT 19% TO 21%
TAX PAID BY STAMPS AFFIXED TO ORIGINAL PACKAGE

NET CONTENTS 1/5 GALLON

Maurice Wine Co.

SAN FRANCISCO

CALIFORNIA

25

Angelica
WINE

ALCOHOLIC STRENGTH NOT UNDER 18% NOR OVER 21% BY VOLUME
TAX PAID BY STAMPS AFFIXED TO CASE

NET CONTENTS   ALCOHOLIC CONTENT
1 HALF GALLON   20% TO 21%

Royal Knight

ANGELICA

Wine 50

BOTTLED BY

Globe Distributing Co.   Los Angeles

PERM. NO. CALIF. 1-368   11th PER. DIST. CALIF.

DRAWN FROM A TAX PAID CONTAINER

TAX PAID BY STAMPS
AFFIXED TO CASE

ALCOHOL 20 %
BY VOLUME

SANTA ALICIA

75 California

Muscatel Wine

BOTTLED FOR
McKESSON & ROBBINS,
INCORPORATED
NEW YORK, N. Y.
PRODUCED AND BOTTLED BY
PADRE VINEYARD COMPANY CUCAMONGA, CALIF.
ONE PINT 8 FL. OZ. · BONDED WINERY No. 1

Sun-Vin BRAND

California

MUSCATEL

ALCOHOL 20% BY VOLUME

NET CONTENTS 1 GALLON

BOTTLED FOR SALE IN CALIFORNIA ONLY, BY

DUMONT WINE DISTRIBUTING CO.

603 H STREET - MODESTO, CALIF.

MANUFACTURED BY

ITALIAN SWISS COLONY

ASTI, CALIFORNIA

LEHMANN, S. F.

WITHDRAWN FROM TAX PAID CONTAINER

SALUTE

ALCOHOL
20%
BY VOLUME

REGINA

REG. U.S. PAT. OFF

California

50

MUSCATEL WINE

TAX PAID
BY STAMPS
AFFIXED
TO CASE

PRODUCED AND BOTTLED BY
ELLENA BROTHERS
ETIWANDA, CALIFORNIA
VINTNERS SINCE 1900

BONDED
WINERY
No. 759

LEHMANN, S. F.

GOLDEN STATE

Wines Co.

Valmont

BRAND

CALIFORNIA

Muscatel

BOTTLED BY
GOLDEN STATE WINES Co.
SAN FRANCISCO, CALIF.
ALCOHOL 20% BY VOLUME

Magic

BRAND

25

California
Muscatel Wine

DISTRIBUTED EXCLUSIVELY BY
KLAUBER WANGENHEIM CO.
LOS ANGELES · SAN DIEGO · EL CENTRO

ALCOHOL 20% BY VOLUME
NET CONTENTS
BOTTLED BY **DISTILLERS OUTLET CO.** LOS ANGELES, CALIF.
WITHDRAWN FROM TAX PAID CONTAINER

LEHMANN, S. F.

NET CONTENTS
1 PINT 8 OZ.

ALCOHOLIC
STRENGTH
20% TO 21%
BY VOLUME

50

Madera
BRAND

CALIFORNIA
WHITE PORT
WINE

MADERA WINERIES & DISTILLERIES
K. ARAKELIAN INC.
MADERA, CALIFORNIA

BONDED
WINERY No. 22

PERMIT
CALIF. No. A-803

11TH PERMISSIVE DISTRICT OF CALIFORNIA
TAX PAID BY STAMPS AFFIXED TO CASE

Don Juan

75

BOTTLED AT
BONDED WINERY
No. 22 - 11TH PERM.
DISTRICT, CALIF.

TAX PAID
BY STAMP AF-
FIXED TO CASE
PERMIT No.
CAL. A 803

NET
CONTENTS
ONE PINT

ALCOHOLIC
STRENGTH 20%
TO 21% BY VOLUME

CALIFORNIA

WHITE PORT

WINE

MADERA WINERIES & DISTILLERIES

K. ARAKELIAN, INC.

MADERA, CALIFORNIA

LEHMANN, S. F.

ALCOHOL 20%
BY VOLUME

NET CONTENTS
ONE QUART

ASTI COLONY

CALIFORNIA

Port

25

BOTTLED BY

ITALIAN SWISS COLONY

ASTI, CALIFORNIA

14th SUP. ADM. DIST. CALIF.　　　BONDED WINERY NO. 1589

TAX PAID BY STAMPS AFFIXED TO CASE

Mission Bell
1930-1932
VINTAGE
ALCOHOLIC
STRENGTH 20%
TO 21% BY VOLUME
75
NET
CONTENTS
½ GALLON
CALIFORNIA
PORT
WINE
MADERA WINERIES & DISTILLERIES
K. ARAKELIAN, INC.
MADERA, CALIFORNIA
LEHMANN, S. F.

SELECTIONS

CALIFORNIA

PORT

Alcohol 20% by Volume

JULIUS LOESER & CO., CHICAGO, ILL.

DISTRIBUTOR

Blended and Bottled by

HAIGH, INC.

B. W. No. 2332

**HEALDSBURG, SONOMA COUNTY
CALIFORNIA**

GUSTO

CALIFORNIA
WINE

NET CONTENTS   ONE GALLON

Port

50

BOTTLED BY
VALLEY VINEYARD CO.
LOS ANGELES, CALIFORNIA
ALCOHOLIC CONTENTS 19½%-21% BY VOLUME
WITHDRAWN FROM TAX PAID CONTAINER

BOTTLED IN CALIFORNIA

BURBANK

T.M. REG. U.S. PAT. OFF.

SPECIAL RESERVE

California

PORT

BOTTLED BY THE BURBANK WINERY - BURBANK, CALIFORNIA

ALCOHOL 20% BY VOLUME

BOTTLED IN CALIFORNIA

Gold Cargo

California

PORT

ALCOHOL
20% BY VOLUME

25

BOTTLED BY
THE BURBANK WINERY
BURBANK · CALIFORNIA

COPR 1935

California Belle

75

CALIFORNIA
PORT
PRODUCED BY **K. ARAKELIAN, INC.** MADERA, CAL.
TRADING AS
MADERA WINERY
BOTTLED BY K. ARAKELIAN, INC., 601 W. 26TH ST., NEW YORK CITY
B. W. NO. 22 - 14TH PERM. DIST. CALIFORNIA   B. S. NO. 379, 2ND PERM. DIST. NEW YORK
TAX PAID BY STAMPS AFFIXED TO CASE
ALCOHOLIC CONTENT 18% - 20% BY VOLUME
N. Y. STATE LIC. NO. DW - 154
NET CONTENTS ONE PINT 8 FL. OZ.

SPECIAL STOCK

BY GOLLY! BUY GALLO!

GALLO

50

CALIFORNIA
PORT

ALCOHOL 20% BY VOLUME

BOTTLED BY
GALLO WINE CO.
LOS ANGELES, CALIF.

PRODUCED BY E. & J. GALLO WINERY
B. W. 4213   MODESTO, CALIF.

THIS WINE
IS MADE FROM
GRAPES RAISED IN
CALIFORNIA PRO-
DUCED SOLELY BY
VINES GROWN
**FROM IMPORTED
CUTTINGS...**
WHICH GRAPES
ARE SELECTED BY
MYSELF FOR THEIR
HIGH QUALITY,
COLOR, SWEET-
NESS AND SOUND-
NESS. THE ENTIRE
OPERATION IS UN-
DER MY PERSONAL
SUPERVISION.
NONE IS GENUINE
WITHOUT MY SIG-
NATURE.

Try Pouring Port
Wine over sugared
strawberries in sher-
bet glasses. Delicious
as an appetizer, des-
sert or punch.

**HOT WINE
PUDDING SAUCE**
½ CUP SUGAR
2 TBSPS. CORN-
STARCH
FEW GRAINS SALT
1 CUP BOILING
WATER
1 INCH STRIP OF
LEMON PEEL
2 TBSPS. LEMON
JUICE
2 TBSPS. BUTTER
¾ CUP CALIFORNIA
PORT WINE

Mix sugar, cornstarch
and salt, add all at
once to boiling water
and lemon peel.
Cook, stirring, until
thick and transpar-
ent. Add lemon juice,
butter and wine.
Heat gently. Serve
hot with steamed
pudding. Add a dash
of nutmeg. Makes 1½
cups sauce, serving
10 to 12.

WEST FARMS
BRAND

CALIFORNIA RUBY PORT
ALCOHOL 20% BY VOLUME
PRODUCED AND BOTTLED AT THE WINERY IN CALIFORNIA BY
ELK GROVE WINERY, INC., ELK GROVE, CALIFORNIA

BOTTLED IN CALIFORNIA

75

20th

CENTURY

CALIFORNIA RUBY PORT

Bottled In California 50

PRODUCED AND BOTTLED
AT THE WINERY BY

CALIFORNIA GROWERS WINERIES
CUTLER, CALIFORNIA

ALCOHOL 20%
BY VOLUME

Royal· ·Lodge

REG. U. S. PAT. OFF.

CALIFORNIA
RUBY PORT
ALCOHOL 20% BY VOLUME

A Rare Wine
ESPECIALLY PACKED
FOR CONNOISSEURS

BOTTLED
IN
CALIFORNIA

PRODUCED AND BOTTLED
AT THE WINERY BY
ELK GROVE WINERY
ELK GROVE, CALIFORNIA

CONTENTS ONE QUART

100
California
Brand

PRODUCED AND BOTTLED IN CALIFORNIA

BY ELK GROVE WINERY, Inc.
ELK GROVE, CALIFORNIA

TAX PAID BY STAMP AFFIXED TO CASE

100
L'Hermitage
Brand

PRODUCED AND BOTTLED AT THE WINERY IN CALIFORNIA
BY   FOR
THE ELK GROVE WINERY INC.   L'HERMITAGE-ELK GROVE
BONDED WINERY No. 3650 · 14TH DIST.
ELK GROVE, CALIFORNIA   ELK GROVE, CALIFORNIA

Two Sisters
BRAND
Reserve Wines

75

PRODUCED AND BOTTLED AT THE
WINERY IN CALIFORNIA BY
ELK GROVE WINERY, Inc.
ELK GROVE, CALIFORNIA

AN
ITALIAN SWISS COLONY
FAMOUS WINE
Pioneer
COLONY
BRAND
50
ITALIAN SWISS COLONY
ASTI, CALIFORNIA
LEHMANN, S.F.
34

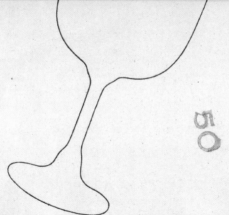

AN
ITALIAN SWISS COLONY
FAMOUS WINE

Early COLONIST

BRAND

LA PALOMA

BRAND

50

LA PALOMA WINERY
A DIVISION OF
ITALIAN SWISS COLONY
CLOVIS - - CALIFORNIA

LEHMANN, S.F.

4 B

★ VICKS ★
DISTRIBUTING COMPANY

Vicks

50

BOTTLED BY
VICKS DISTRIBUTING CO.
OAKLAND, CALIFORNIA
WITHDRAWN FROM TAX PAID CONTAINER

ITALIAN SWISS COLONY

100

ITALIAN SWISS COLONY

100

LEHMANN, S.F. 99

ITALIAN SWISS COLONY

25

LEHMANN, S.F. 100

GRAPE PRESS

BRAND

25

LEHMANN S. F.

ALCOHOLIC STRENGTH 20% BY VOLUME

ALTAVALE
WINES

TAX PAID BY STAMPS AFFIXED TO CASE

THE E.G. LYONS & RAAS COMPANY
SAN FRANCISCO   CALIFORNIA
BONDED WINERY NO. 3674   14TH PERM. DIST. CAL.

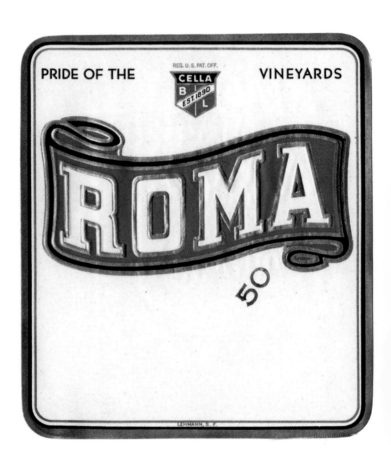

PRIDE OF THE — REG. U.S. PAT. OFF. CELLA B EST.1890 L — VINEYARDS

ROMA

50

LEHMANN, S. F.

TROCHA

BRAND

CALIFORNIA

Olde Gotham

BRAND

50

Bottled In California

PRODUCED AND BOTTLED AT THE WINERY BY

ELK GROVE WINERY, INC.

ELK GROVE
CALIFORNIA

18 K

T. M. REG. U.S. PAT. OFF.

CALIFORNIA

50

AN
ITALIAN SWISS COLONY
FAMOUS WINE

ITALIAN COLONY
BRAND

25

ITALIAN SWISS COLONY
ASTI, CALIFORNIA

CAL-STATE

ESTABLISHED 1893
QUALITY WINES

E.V.P.

California

50

Topper

CALIFORNIA

25

WINE

PRODUCED AND BOTTLED BY
B. CRIBARI & SONS, Inc.
MADRONE, CALIF.
BONDED WINERY No. 164

Cool Arbor

CALIFORNIA

25

ENCORE

CALIFORNIA

25

Smil-O

T. M. REG. BY A. JOSEPH

from **CALIFORNIA**

MANUFACTURED BY **TULARE WINERY CO.** TULARE CALIFORNIA